A Community Shakespeare Company
Edition of

A Midsummer Night's Dream

Original verse adaptation by
Richard Carter

"Enriching young lives, cultivating community"

Other original verse adaptations by Richard Carter,
available through iUniverse:

As You Like It

The Comedy Of Errors

The Taming Of The Shrew

The Two Gentlemen Of Verona

A Community Shakespeare Company
Edition of

A Midsummer Night's Dream

Original verse adaptation by

Richard Carter

"Enriching young lives, cultivating community"

iUniverse, Inc.
New York Lincoln Shanghai

A Community Shakespeare Company Edition of
A Midsummer Night's Dream

iUniverse books may be ordered through booksellers or by contacting:

iUniverse
2021 Pine Lake Road, Suite 100
Lincoln, NE 68512
www.iuniverse.com
1-800-Authors (1-800-288-4677)

Because of the dynamic nature of the Internet, any Web addresses or links contained in this book may have changed since publication and may no longer be valid.

The views expressed in this work are solely those of the author and do not necessarily reflect the views of the publisher, and the publisher hereby disclaims any responsibility for them.

ISBN: 978-0-595-48343-3 (pbk)
ISBN: 978-0-595-60433-3 (ebk)

Printed in the United States of America

CONTENTS

CAST OF CHARACTERS

THESEUS	duke of Athens
HYPPOLYTA	queen of the Amazons, betrothed to Theseus
EGEUS	a nobleman, Hermia's father
HERMIA	in love with Lysander
HELENA	in love with Demetrius
LYSANDER, DEMETRIUS	young noblemen
PHILOSTRATE	Master of the Revels at Theseus' court
OBERON	king of the fairies
TITANIA	queen of the fairies
PUCK	a mischievous fairy
FIRST FAIRY	meets Puck in the wood
PEASBLOSSOM, COBWEB, MOTH, MUSTARDSEED	fairies
PETER QUINCE	a carpenter
NICK BOTTOM	a weaver
FRANCIS FLUTE	a bellows-mender
TOM SNOUT	a tinker
SNUG	a joiner
ROBIN STARVELING	a tailor
ATTENDANTS	at the court of Theseus
FAIRIES	attending on Oberon and Titania

This play should run between 80 and 90 minutes, without intermission

ACT I, scene 1

(ATHENS: THE PALACE OF THESEUS. ENTER THESEUS, HIPPOLYTA, PHILOSTRATE, ATTENDANTS) *Royal music*

THESEUS
Now, fair Hippolyta, our nuptial hour draws on soon,
Four happy days bring in another moon;
But O methinks, how slow the old moon wanes,
Like a step-dame or a dowager, doddering with her canes.

HIPPOLYTA
Four days will quickly steep themselves in night;
Four nights will quickly, like dreams, take flight,
And then the new moon, like a silver bow bent on high
Shall behold the night of our solemnities draw nigh.

THESEUS
Go, Philostrate, stir up the Athenian youth;
Awake the pert and nimble spirit of their mirth.

(EXIT PHILOSTRATE. ENTER EGEUS, HERMIA, LYSANDER, AND DEMETRIUS)

EGEUS
Happy be Theseus, renownèd duke!

THESEUS
Good Egeus, what's the news?

EGEUS
My daughter makes me puke!
Full of vexation, with complaint against my child,
Come I before your grace: Hermia drives me wild!
Stand forth, Demetrius: my noble lord, *this* man
Hath my consent to marry her. Say, Demetrius.

DEMETRIUS
That's the plan.

EGEUS
Stand forth, Lysander: gracious duke, *this* ignoble youth
Hath bewitched my child. Say, Demetrius.

DEMETRIUS
That's the truth.

EGEUS
With feigning voice, with rhymes of love, with bracelets of thy hair,
Thou, *thou* Lysander, hast stolen this treasure most rare:
Thou hast *filched* my daughter's heart with your cunning moonlight verses,
Turned obedience to stubborn harshness; earned a father's curses!
My gracious duke, before your grace, I beg the ancient right:
The privilege of Athens says I may dispose of her as I might.
As she is mine, I give her to Demetrius with my last breath,
Or according to our law she goes immediately to her death.

THESEUS
What say you, Hermia? Be advised, your father is your lord,
And you but a form in wax, to be imprinted with his word.
Demetrius is a worthy gentleman.

HERMIA
So is Lysander.

THESEUS
That's true;
But lacking your father's voice, he's the lesser. Come, pay your father his due.

HERMIA
I would my father looked with *my* eyes.

THESEUS
Rather *your* eyes must *his* judgment seek.

HERMIA
I do entreat your pardon: I can't be married to this *geek*!
I know not how I'm made so bold to plead to your grace,
But I beseech you, tell me the worst that may befall me in this case:
If I refuse to wed Demetrius?

THESEUS
Either die, or give up the society of men;
Live barren, see man nevermore.

HERMIA
Not even now and then?

THESEUS
Blessed are they that master their blood in the livery of a nun,
Chanting faint hymns to the cold fruitless moon, if that's your idea of fun.

HERMIA
So will I live, so die, my lord, before I yield myself to *this* man.

THESEUS
Take time to pause, and by the new moon, be certain of your plan:
For upon that day, when my Amazonian love and I shall be wed,
You must prepare to die, or to take Demetrius to your bed,
Or else to live a single life, withering on the virgin thorn;
Earthlier happy is the rose distilled, whose scent is thus reborn.

DEMETRIUS
Relent, sweet Hermia! Lysander, yield! Your passion is just a whim.

LYSANDER
You have her *father's* love, Demetrius: let you marry him.

EGEUS
Scornful Lysander! True, he hath my love, and with it my estate:
As she is mine, I give her to Demetrius.

HERMIA
Urrgh! You know I hate
Him.

LYSANDER
(TO THESEUS) My lord, I am as well derived as he, my fortunes equal;
What's more, I am beloved of Hermia. For Demetrius, she's just the sequel:
He woo'd Nedar's daughter Helena, and won her: hook, line and sinker.
She *dotes* upon this inconstant man!

HERMIA
I told you he's a stinker.

THESEUS
I confess, I have heard this tale, but my mind being full, did forget.
Demetrius, come, and Egeus too, we'll have some private talk yet.
For you, fair Hermia, arm yourself: fit your fancies to your father's will,
Or the law of Athens yields you to death, or to the nunnery still.

(EXEUNT ALL EXCEPT LYSANDER AND HERMIA)

LYSANDER
How now, my love? How chance the roses in thy cheek do fade so fast?
The course of true love never did run smooth in any tale from the past.

HERMIA
If then true lovers have ever been crossed, it is our destiny too.
We must have patience and bear our cross, and so pay Love its due.

LYSANDER
A good persuasion. Therefore, hear me, Hermia: I have a dowager aunt.
She hath no child; a house seven leagues from Athens is her haunt.
She respects me as her only son, to *her* house we may flee,
Where the Athenian law cannot pursue us: *there* may I marry thee.
Steal forth from thy father's house tomorrow night, and meet me in the wood,
Where once I met thee with Helena; I'll wait where then I stood.

HERMIA
My good Lysander, I swear to thee by Cupid's strongest bow,
In that same place will I meet thee. Tomorrow will I go!

LYSANDER
Keep promise, love. Look, here comes Helena.

(ENTER HELENA)

HERMIA
Fair Helena! Whither away?

HELENA
Call you *me* fair? O Hermia, that fair again unsay.

Demetrius loves *your* fair. Sickness is catching, why is not *favor* so?
Yours would I catch, fair Hermia, willingly ere I go.
My ear should catch your voice, my eye your eye,
My tongue should speak as *yours* when Demetrius is nigh.
Teach me how you look, and with what art
You sway the motion of Demetrius' heart.

HERMIA
I frown upon him, yet he loves me still.

HELENA
O that your frowns would teach my smiles such skill!

HERMIA
I give him curses, yet he gives me love.

HELENA
O that my prayers could such affection move!

HERMIA
The more I hate, the more he follows me.

HELENA
The more I love, the more he hateth me.

HERMIA
His folly, Helena, is no fault of mine.

HELENA
None but your beauty: would *that* fault were mine.

HERMIA
Take comfort: he no more shall see my face;
Lysander and myself will fly this place.

LYSANDER
Helen, to you our minds we will unfold.
Tomorrow night, when the waning moon you do behold—
A time that lovers' flights doth still conceal—
Through Athens' gates have we devised to steal.

HERMIA

And in the wood, where you and I were wont to meet,
Emptying our hearts of their counsel sweet,
There Lysander and I shall take flight,
And thence from Athens turn away our sight.
Farewell, sweet playfellow: pray thou for us;
And good luck grant thee thy Demetrius.

(EXIT HERMIA)

LYSANDER

Till tomorrow, my Hermia! Helena, adieu:
As you on him, Demetrius dote on you.

(EXIT LYSANDER)

HELENA

How happy some o'er other some can be!
Through Athens I am thought as fair as she;
But what of that? *Demetrius* thinks not so;
He sees *not* what all but he do know!
I will go tell him of fair Hermia's flight,
Then to the wood will he tomorrow night:
I'll lead him, and for this most welcome news,
He may yet thank me, and so change his views.
Herein mean I to enrich mine own lot,
To have the love back again, which he hath forgot.

(EXIT)

ACT I, scene 2

(ATHENS: PETER QUINCE'S HOUSE. ENTER QUINCE, SNUG, BOTTOM, FLUTE, SNOUT, AND STARVELING) *elavilope music?*

QUINCE
Is all our company here?

BOTTOM
You were best to call them man by man.

QUINCE
(WITH A SCROLL)
Here is the name of every man in Athens thought fit for our plan:
We play before the duke and duchess on their wedding night.

BOTTOM
First, good Peter Quince, say what play will greet their sight.

QUINCE
The most lamentable comedy, and most cruel death of Pyramus and Thisbe.

BOTTOM
Now call each actor by the scroll, and say which part will *his* be.

QUINCE
Nick Bottom, the weaver?

BOTTOM
Ready! Name what I am for, and proceed.

QUINCE
You, Nick Bottom, are set down for Pyramus.

BOTTOM
What is he? A lover?

QUINCE
Indeed.
A lover that kills himself most gallant for love.

BOTTOM
Let the audience look to their eyes: storms of tears will I move!
The raging rocks avenges son
And shivering shocks
Shall break the locks ...
This was lofty!

QUINCE
Francis Flute, the bellows-mender?

FLUTE
Here, Peter Quince.

QUINCE
You must take Thisbe.

FLUTE
What is Thisbe? A wandering knight, or a prince?

QUINCE
It is the lady that Pyramus loves.

FLUTE
Nay, faith, I'm growing a beard!
Let me not play a woman.

QUINCE
You'll be in a mask.

FLUTE
That's weird.

BOTTOM
If I may hide my face, let me play Thisbe too!
I'll speak in a monstrous little voice: "Oh Thisne, Thisne, I love you!"

QUINCE
No, you must play Pyramus; Flute is Thisbe. Starveling is Thisbe's mother.
Pyramus' father is Snout. The lion is Snug.

ALL BUT SNUG
Oh, brother!

SNUG
Have you the lion's part written? Pray give it me, for I am slow.

QUINCE
It is nothing but roaring.

BOTTOM
Let *me* play the lion! I will roar till I stop the show!
(ROARS)

STARVELING
If you do it too terribly, you will fright the ladies.

SNOUT
And then they will hang us all.

BOTTOM
Then I'll roar as gently as a sucking dove. Like a nightingale will I call.
(ROARS SWEETLY)

QUINCE
You can play no part but Pyramus.

BOTTOM
Well, I will undertake it.

ALL
Amen.

BOTTOM
What beard were I best to play it in?

SNOUT
Oy!

STARVELING
Here we go again.

BOTTOM

I will play it in either your straw-color beard, orange-tawny, or purple-in-grain.

QUINCE

Masters, here are your parts. Tomorrow we meet: con your lines by then.
We rehearse by moonlight, in the palace wood, a mile without the town,
For if we meet in the city, our devices shall be known.

BOTTOM

We will meet, and there we may rehearse most obscenely, courageously too.
Enough, hold or cut bow-strings: take pains, be perfect; adieu!

(EXEUNT)

ACT II, scene 1

(A WOOD NEAR ATHENS. ENTER 1ST FAIRY, & PUCK ON THE OTHER SIDE) *woods* *magic*

<u>PUCK</u>
How now, spirit! Whither wander you?

<u>1ST FAIRY</u>
Over hill, over dale
Through bush, through brier
Over park, over pale,
Through flood, through fire,
I do wander everywhere,
Swifter than the moon's sphere;
And I serve the fairy queen,
To dew her orbs upon the green.
Farewell, thou spirit, I'll be gone;
Our queen and her elves come here anon.

<u>PUCK</u>
The king doth keep his revels here tonight.
Take heed the queen come not within his sight;
For Oberon is full of wrath
Because *she* as attendant hath
A lovely boy, stolen from an Indian king,
And jealous Oberon would have the changeling.

<u>1ST FAIRY</u>
Either I mistake your shape and making quite,
Or else you are that shrewd and knavish sprite
Called Robin Goodfellow; are you not he
That frights the maidens of the villagery,
Misleads night-wanderers, laughing at their plight,
Who, "Hobgoblin" call you, and "Sweet Puck," am I not right?

<u>PUCK</u>
Thou speak'st aright;
I am that merry wanderer of the night.
I jest to Oberon, and make him smile

When I a fat and bean-fed horse beguile,
Neighing in likeness of a filly foal;
And sometime lurk I in a gossip's bowl,
In very likeness of a roasted crab,
And when she drinks, against her lips I bob.
The wisest aunt, sometime for a stool mistaketh me;
Then slip I from her bum, and down topples she!
But room, fairy! Here comes Oberon.

1ST FAIRY
And here my mistress. Would that he were gone!

(THEY STEP ASIDE. ENTER OBERON FROM ONE SIDE, WITH HIS
ATTENDANTS; AND TITANIA FROM THE OTHER, WITH HERS.)

OBERON
Ill met by moonlight, proud Titania fair.

TITANIA
Jealous Oberon! Fairies, haste over there;
Skip hence, I have forsworn his bed and board.

OBERON
Tarry, rash wanton! Am not I thy lord?

TITANIA
Then I must be thy lady. But well I know
When thou away from Fairlyland dost go,
Versing love and playing on pipes of corn
To the amorous shepherdess, or the bouncing Amazon!
Your warrior love, Hippolyta will soon be wed,
To Theseus, and *you* must give joy to *their* wedding bed.

OBERON
How canst thou thus rail, Titania, for shame,
Knowing *thy* love to Theseus; I know your game.

TITANIA
These are words of jealousy, and well you know
That never since the middle summer's glow,
Met we on hill, in forest, or by sea,

To dance our ringlets to the wind most free,
But with *thy* brawls thou hast disturbed our sport!
Therefore the winds, piping in retort,
Have sucked contagious fogs upon the land;
Each pelting river made to overflow its sand,
Till the fold stands empty in the drownèd field—
The ploughman lost his sweat—for no green corn will it yield;
The ox hath therefore stretched his yoke in vain,
From our debate, Oberon: you're a pain.

OBERON
It lies in you to fix it then, my fawn:
Why should Titania cross her Oberon?
I do but beg the changeling boy.

TITANIA
Not for all Fairyland.

OBERON
Don't be coy.

TITANIA
His mother served me in the spiced Indian air;
By night, full often hath she gossiped in mine ear,
But she, being mortal, of bearing that boy did die.
For her sake do I rear him up; now you know why.

OBERON
Give me that boy as page, and I will dance in your round.

TITANIA
Not for thy fairy kingdom! Fairies, let us leave this ground.
We shall chide downright, if I longer stay!

(EXIT TITANIA WITH HER ATTENDANTS)

OBERON
Well, Titania, go thy way.
Thou shalt not from this grove till I tor*ment* thee;
Come, gentle Puck, for this purpose heaven sent thee.
I once saw Cupid, all armèd with his bow,

Flying between the cold moon and the earth below;
He loosed his love-shaft at a virgin by the sea,
But missed his mark, and she passed on, fancy free.
Yet marked *I* where the bolt of Cupid fell,
Upon a western flower in the dell:
"Love-in-idleness" maidens call it in their bower,
I showed it thee once; fetch me that flower.
The juice of it, on sleeping eyelids laid,
Will make one madly dote, man or maid,
On the next live creature that meets the eye.

PUCK
I'll put a girdle round the earth in forty minutes.

(EXIT PUCK)

OBERON
Fly!
Having once this juice, I'll watch Titania sleeping,
And drop the liquor in her eyes, like gentle weeping.
When she wakes, what she sees—beast, fowl or flunky—
She shall pursue, be it bear, bull or monkey!
Ere I take this charm from off her sight,
I'll make her render up her page to my right.
But who comes here? I am invisible to their eyes,
And will overhear their conference in this disguise.

(ENTER DEMETRIUS, HELENA FOLLOWING HIM)

DEMETRIUS
I love thee not, therefore pursue me not.
Where is Lysander? Where fair Hermia: she's hot!
Thou told'st me they were stolen unto this wood,
And here am I, though it does me no good
Because I cannot find Hermia. Hence, get thee gone!

HELENA
Hard-hearted Demetrius, you draw me on.

DEMETRIUS
Do I entice you? Do I speak you fair?
Or do I not in truth most rare,
Tell you I do not, *cannot* love you full sore?

HELENA
And even for that, I love you the more.
I am your spaniel: the more you spurn me,
The more faithful the fire of my love will burn me.

DEMETRIUS
Tempt not too much the hatred of my spirit,
For I am sick when I look on you, and you must hear it.

HELENA
And *I* am sick when I look *not* upon you.

DEMETRIUS
I'll leave thee to the mercy of wild beasts in this zoo.

HELENA
The wildest hath not such a heart as your own:
Run where you will: I'm your dog, you're my bone!

DEMETRIUS
Let me go: if you follow me, it will do you no good,
I shall do thee mischief in this wood.

HELENA
Aye, in the temple, the town, the field,
You do me mischief, Demetrius. Yield!
Women cannot fight for love, as men may do;
We should be woo'd, and were not made to woo.
(EXIT DEMETRIUS)
I'll follow thee and make a heaven of hell,
To die upon the hand I love so well.

(EXIT HELENA)

OBERON
Fare thee well, nymph. Ere he do leave this grove,

Thou shalt fly *him*, and *he* shall seek *thy* love.
(ENTER PUCK)
Welcome wanderer, hast thou the flower?
Pray, give it me; I'll unlock its power.
I know a bank where the wild thyme blows,
Where oxslips and the nodding violet grows:
There sleeps Titania some time of the night,
Lulled in these flowers with dances of delight.
With the juice of this flower I'll streak her eyes,
And make her full of hateful fantasies.
(TO PUCK) Take thou some of it, and seek through this grove:
A sweet Athenian lady is in love
With a disdainful youth: anoint his eyes;
But do it when the next thing that he espies
May be the lady. Thou shalt know the man
By the Athenian garments he hath on.
Look thou meet me ere the first cock crow.

PUCK
Fear not, my lord, your servant shall do so.

(EXEUNT)

ACT II, scene 2

(ANOTHER PART OF THE WOOD. ENTER TITANIA WITH HER ATTEN-
DANTS)

TITANIA
Come, now a roundel and a fairy song,
Keep back the owl that nightly hoots along.
Sing me asleep, and do thy best,
Then to your offices, and let me rest.

(THE FAIRIES SING AND DANCE)

SONG
You spotted snakes with double tongue,
Thorny hedgehogs, be not seen;
Newts and blind-worms, do no wrong,
Come not near our fairy queen.
Lulla, lulla, lullaby; lulla, lulla, lullaby.
Weaving spiders come not here;
Hence you long-legged spinners, hence!
Beetles black, approach not near;
Worm nor snail, do no offence.
Lulla, lulla, lullaby; lulla, lulla, lullaby.

1ST FAIRY
Hence, away! Now all is well.
One aloof stand sentinel.

(EXEUNT FAIRIES. TITANIA SLEEPS. ENTER OBERON, AND SQUEEZES
THE FLOWER ON TITANIA'S EYELIDS)

OBERON
What thou seest when thou dost wake,
Do it for thy true-love take;
Be it hedgehog, cat, or bear,
Dog, or boar with bristled hair,
In thy eye, whate're appear,
When thou wak'st, it is thy dear.

Wake when some vile thing is near.

(EXIT OBERON. ENTER LYSANDER AND HERMIA)

LYSANDER
Fair love, you faint with wandering in the wood;
We'll rest us, Hermia, if you think it good,
And tarry for the comfort of the day,
For to speak the truth, I have forgot our way.

HERMIA
Be it so, Lysander: find you out a bed,
For upon this bank I will rest my head.

LYSANDER
One turf shall serve as pillow for us both.

HERMIA
Nay, good Lysander, for my sake, lie further off;
Such separation as may well be said
Becomes a virtuous bachelor and a maid,
So far be distant; and, good night, sweet friend.
Thy love ne'er alter till thy sweet life end!

LYSANDER
(MOVES AWAY A LITTLE DISTANCE)
Here is my bed: sleep give thee all his rest.

HERMIA
With half that wish, the wisher's eyes be pressed.

(THEY SLEEP. ENTER PUCK)

PUCK
Through the forest I have gone,
But Athenian found I none,
On whose eyes I might approve
This flower's force in stirring love.
Night and silence! who is here?
Weeds of Athens he doth wear:
This is he my master said

Despisèd the Athenian maid;
And here the maiden, sleeping sound
On the dank and dirty ground.
Pretty soul! she durst not lie
Near this lack-love, this kill-courtesy.
(SQUEEZES THE FLOWER ON LYSANDER'S EYELIDS)
Churl, upon thy eyes I throw
All the power this charm doth owe.
When thou wak'st, let love consume
Thy sleepless eyes: va-va-va voom!
So awake when I am gone,
For I must now to Oberon.

(EXIT PUCK. ENTER DEMETRIUS AND HELENA, RUNNING)

HELENA
Stay, though thou kill me, sweet Demetrius!

DEMETRIUS
I charge thee hence, and do not haunt me thus.

HELENA
O wilt thou darkling leave me? Do not so.

DEMETRIUS
Stay, on thy peril: I alone will go.

(EXIT DEMETRIUS)

HELENA
O, I am out of breath in this fond chase.
The more my prayer, the lesser is my grace.
Happy is Hermia, wheresoe'er she lies;
For she hath blessèd and attractive eyes
Whilst I, methinks, am as ugly as a bear,
For beasts that meet me run away in fear!
Therefore no marvel that Demetrius
Do as a monster fly my presence thus.
But who is here? Lysander! on the ground!
Dead? or asleep? I see no blood, no wound.

Lysander, if you live, good sir, awake.

LYSANDER
(WAKING) And run through fire will I for thy sweet sake.
Transparent Helena! Nature shows her art
That with new eyes, all at once, I see thy heart.
Where is Demetrius? O how fit a word
Is that vile name to perish on my sword.

HELENA
Do not say so, Lysander, say not so.
Though he love Hermia, Hermia loves *you*.
Be content.

LYSANDER
Content with Hermia! No, I do repent
The tedious minutes with her I've spent.
Not Hermia but Helena I love:
Who will not change a raven for a dove?

HELENA
Wherefore was I to this keen mockery born?
When at your hands did I deserve this scorn?
Is't not enough, not enough, young man,
That I did never, no, nor never can
Deserve a sweet look from Demetrius' eye,
But you must flout my insufficiency?
Good troth, you do me wrong—good sooth, you do—
In such disdainful manner me to woo.
But fare you well. Perforce I must confess
I thought you lord of more true gentleness.
O, that a lady of one man refused
Should of another therefore be abused.

(EXIT HELENA)

LYSANDER
She sees not Hermia. Hermia, sleep thou there;
And never mayst thou come Lysander near.
For, as too much of the sweetest things,

Deep loathing to the stomach brings,
So thou, my too-sweet lover be
Of all things hated, but most of me!
And, all my powers, address your love and might
To honor Helen, and to be her knight.

(EXIT LYSANDER)

HERMIA
(WAKING) Help me, Lysander! Help! Do thy best
To pluck this crawling serpent from my breast!
Aye me, for pity! What a dream was here!
Lysander, look how I do quake with fear!
Methought a serpent ate my heart away,
And you sat smiling at his cruel prey.
Lysander! what, removed? Lysander! lord!
Out of hearing? Gone? No sound, no word?
Alack, where are you? Speak an if you hear;
Speak, of all loves! I swoon almost with fear.
No? Then I will perceive you are not nigh:
Either death or you I'll find immediately.

(EXIT)

ACT III, scene 1

(THE WOOD. TITANIA LIES ASLEEP. ENTER QUINCE, SNUG, BOTTOM, FLUTE, SNOUT, AND STARVELING)

BOTTOM
Are we all met?

QUINCE
Here's a marvelous convenient place
For our rehearsal; this green plot of space
Shall be our stage, and we will do it
As before the duke: now, let us run through it.

BOTTOM
Peter Quince!

QUINCE
What sayest thou, bully Bottom?

BOTTOM
There are things in this play that won't please, but I've caught 'em:
First, Pyramus must kill himself, which ladies cannot abide.

STARVELING
Then we must leave the killing out.

SNUG
Aye, leave the killing aside.

BOTTOM
Not a whit: I have a device to make all well.
Write me a prologue, and let the prologue tell
That Pyramus is not to be killed in real life.
For better assurance, and to mend all strife,
Say that I, Pyramus, am but Bottom the weaver,
This will put out them out of fear.

FLUTE
(ASIDE) He's a busy beaver.

SNOUT
(ASIDE) Aye, he finds out problems we've got to fix.

QUINCE
We'll have such a prologue; let it be written in eight and six.

STARVELING
Will not the ladies be afraid of the lion?

SNUG
I fear it, I promise you: I'll make them start cryin'.

BOTTOM
A lion among ladies is sure to be fearful,
A dreadful thing.

SNOUT
We must not make them tearful.

FLUTE
Therefore another prologue must tell he's no beast.

BOTTOM
Nay, but name his name, and show half his face at least,
Through the lion's neck; and let him speak thus:
"Ladies," or "Fair ladies, there's no need to fuss:
I entreat you not to tremble, there's no need to fear,
For I am a man, as other men here."
And tell them plainly you're the joiner, Snug.

QUINCE
It shall be so.

BOTTOM
There's no sweeping a lion under the rug.

QUINCE
But there are two hard things yet, to stage our play,
For Pyramus and Thisbe meet not by day.
How bring we moonlight indoors, I would know.

SNOUT
Doth the moon not shine on the night of our show?

BOTTOM
A calendar! Find out moonshine, I say.

QUINCE
It doth shine that night.

FLUTE
Then let it shine on our play.

BOTTOM
Leave a casement of the great chamber window full wide,
That the moonlight may shine on our acting inside!

QUINCE
Or else, one might come in the *person* of the moon,
Bearing a lantern.

BOTTOM
Nay: he'd look like a goon.

STARVELING
No more than the lion, with his face through his neck.

SNUG
I'm not a goon!

STARVELING
Nor I!

BOTTOM
(SHRUGS) What the heck.

QUINCE
There's one more thing: we must present a wall,
For through it, Pyramus and Thisbe must call.

SNOUT
You can never bring in a wall.

FLUTE
Bottom, what do you think?

BOTTOM
Some man must *present* the Wall, and his fingers, the chink,
Through which the lovers whisper their hearts.

QUINCE
Then all is well. Come, sit down and rehearse your parts.

(ENTER PUCK)

PUCK
What hempen homespuns have we here,
With the cradle of the fairy queen so near?
What, a play? I'll be an auditor; and an actor, perhaps,
If I see cause to confuse these chaps.

QUINCE
Speak, Pyramus! Thisbe: stand forth so you may meet.

BOTTOM
Thisbe, the flowers of odious savors sweet—

QUINCE
Odorous, odorous!

BOTTOM
—odors savors sweet:
So hath thy breath my dearest Thisbe dear.
But hark a voice! I'll be back, you stay right here.

(EXIT BOTTOM)

PUCK
A stranger Pyramus than e'er played since.
I'll after him.

(EXIT PUCK)

FLUTE
Must I speak now, Peter Quince?

QUINCE
Aye, through the wall, you must find the crack,
He's but gone to find the noise he heard; he's coming back.

FLUTE
Most radiant Pyramus, like red rose on triumphant brier,
As true as truest horse that yet would never tire,
I'll meet thee, Pyramus at Ninny's tomb.

QUINCE
Ninus' tomb! You must not speak that yet;
That you answer to Pyramus. Don't forget!
Pyramus, you missed your cue: it was "*never tire*"

FLUTE
As true as truest horse, that yet would never tire.
(NOTE: THIS LINE MAY BE REPEATED, AS NEEDED, TO GIVE BOTTOM
TIME TO CHANGE)

(ENTER PUCK, AND BOTTOM WEARING AN ASS'S HEAD)

BOTTOM
Thisbe! I were only thine, if I were fair.

QUINCE
O monstrous! O strange! We're haunted! Fly masters! Help!

(EXEUNT ALL EXCEPT BOTTOM AND PUCK)

PUCK
Now that's what I call an entrance. Go on, yelp,
I'll follow you, lead you round and about,
With a neigh, and a bark, and a grunt, and a shout!

(EXIT PUCK)

BOTTOM
Why do they run away? This is knavery to fright me.

They'll sneak up on me now, to grab me or bite me.

(ENTER SNOUT)

SNOUT
O Bottom, thou art changed! What do I see on thee?

BOTTOM
An ass-head of your own? You'll not make a fool of me.

(EXIT SNOUT. ENTER QUINCE)

QUINCE
Bless thee, Bottom! Bless thee! Thou art translated!

(EXIT QUINCE)

BOTTOM
I see their knavery: they won't be sated
Until they make an *ass* of me!
But I'll not stir from this place, they'll see.
I'll walk up and down, I'll sing! They shall hear.
I'm not afraid, for there's nothing to fear.
(SINGS) *The ousel cock, so black of hue,*
With orange-tawny bill,
The throstle with his note so true,
The wren with little quill—

TITANIA
(WAKING) What angel wakes me from my flowery den?
I pray thee gentle mortal, sing again!

BOTTOM
The finch, the sparrow, and the lark,
The plain-song cuckoo gray,
Whose note full many a man doth mark,
And dares not answer "Nay."

TITANIA
Mine ear is much enamored of thy note,
So is mine eye of thy shape, that I might dote;

And thy fair virtue's force indeed doth move me
On first view to say, to swear, that I do love thee!

BOTTOM
Methinks, mistress, you should have little reason for that.
And yet, to say truth, like cur and cat,
Reason and love keep little company nowadays.

TITANIA
Thou art as wise as thou art beautiful in my gaze.

BOTTOM
Not so, neither; for I've a sudden craving for grass.
If I could find my way home, I would not feel such an ass.

TITANIA
Out of this wood do not desire to go:
Thou shalt remain here, whether thou wilt or no.
I am a spirit of no common rate;
The summer still doth tend upon my state;
And I do love thee; therefore go with me.
I'll give thee fairies to attend on thee,
And I will purge thy mortal grossness so
That thou shalt like an airy spirit go.
Peaseblossom, Cobweb, Moth, and Mustardseed!

(ENTER FOUR FAIRIES)

PEASEBLOSSOM
Ready.

COBWEB
And I.

MOTH
And I.

MUSTARDSEED
And I.

PEASEBLOSSOM
Hail, mortal!

COBWEB
Hail!

MOTH
Hail!

MUSTARDSEED
Hail!

BOTTOM
I cry your worships mercy, most heartily.
I beseech *your* worship's name: pray give it me.

COBWEB
Cobweb.

BOTTOM
Master Cobweb, I shall desire more acquaintance with you.
And honest fairy, may I have *your* name too?

PEASEBLOSSOM
Peaseblossom.

BOTTOM
Commend me to your mother, Mistress Squash,
And to your father, Master Peascod; I'm only joshing.
And *your* name?

MOTH
Moth.

BOTTOM
And *yours?*

MUSTARDSEED
Mustardseed.

BOTTOM
Master Mustardseed, I know your patience well:

The giant ox-beef dwelling in the dell
Hath many a gentleman of your house devoured,
Made my eyes water for your kindred. The beast! He's a coward.

TITANIA

Come, wait upon him; lead him to my bower.
The moon, methinks weeps, so weeps every little flower,
Lamenting some enforcèd chastity.
Tie up my love's tongue, bring him silently.

(EXEUNT)

ACT III, scene 2

(ANOTHER PART OF THE WOOD. ENTER OBERON)

OBERON
I wonder if Titania be awaked? What was it next came in her eye,
Which she must dote on in extremity?
(ENTER PUCK)
How now, mad spirit! What business haunts this grove?

PUCK
My mistress with a monster is in love!
Near to her close and consecrated bower,
While she was in her dull and sleeping hour,
A crew of patches, rude mechanicals,
That work for bread upon Athenian stalls,
Were met together to rehearse a play,
Intended for great Theseus' nuptial day.
The shallowest thick-skin of that barren sort,
Who Pyramus presented in their sport,
Forsook his scene and entered in a brake;
When I did him at this advantage take,
An ass's nole I fixed upon his head.
Anon his Thisbe must be answerèd,
And forth my mimic comes: when they him spy,
So at his sight away his fellows fly!
I led them on in this distracted fear,
And left sweet Pyramus translated there;
When in that moment, so it came to pass,
Titania waked, and straightway loved an ass.

OBERON
This falls out better than I could devise!
But hast thou latched the Athenian's eyes
With the love-juice, as I bid thee do?

PUCK
I took him sleeping—that is finished too;
And the Athenian woman by his side,

That when he waked, of force she must be eyed.

(ENTER DEMETRIUS AND HERMIA)

OBERON
Stand close: this is the same Athenian.

PUCK
This is the woman; but not this the man.

DEMETRIUS
O why rebuke you him that loves you so?
Lay such bitter breath on your bitter foe.

HERMIA
I but chide; but I should use thee worse,
For thou, I fear hast given me cause to curse:
If thou has slain Lysander in his sleep,
You're in deep doo-doo, Mister; I mean deep!
The sun was not so true unto the day
As he to me. Would he have stolen away
From sleeping Hermia? Not!
The moon would sooner leave the earth, you sot!
It cannot be but thou hast murdered him;
So should a murderer look, so dead, so grim.

DEMETRIUS
So should the murdered look, and so should I,
Pierced through the heart with your stern cruelty.
Yet you, the murderer, look as bright, as clear,
As yonder Venus in her glimmering sphere.

HERMIA
What's this to my Lysander? Where is he?
Ah, good Demetrius, wilt thou give him me?

DEMETRIUS
I had rather give his carcass to my hounds.

HERMIA
Out, dog! out, cur! You drive me past the bounds

Of maiden's patience. Hast thou slain him then?
Henceforth be never numbered among men!

DEMETRIUS
You waste your words to drag me through the mud:
I am not guilty of Lysander's blood,
Nor is he dead, for aught that I can tell.

HERMIA
I pray thee, tell me then that he is well.

DEMETRIUS
And if I could, what should I get therefore?

HERMIA
A privilege—never to see me more.
And from thy hated presence part I so;
See me no more, whether he be dead or no.

(EXIT HERMIA)

DEMETRIUS
There is no following her in this fierce vein:
Here therefore for a while I will remain.
If as she says: I'm in the "doo-doo deep,"
When a woman runs amuck, a man should sleep.
(LIES DOWN AND SLEEPS)

OBERON
What hast thou done? Thou hast mistaken quite,
And laid the love-juice on some *true* love's sight.
About the wood go swifter than the wind,
And Helena of Athens look thou find:
All fancy-sick she is, and pale of cheer,
With sighs of love, that cost the fresh blood dear.
By some illusion see thou bring her here.
I'll charm his eyes for when she do appear.

PUCK
I go, I go—look how I go—
Swifter than arrow from the Tartar's bow.

(EXIT PUCK)

OBERON
Flower of this purple dye
Hit with Cupid's archery,
Sink in apple of his eye
(SQUEEZES THE FLOWER ON DEMETRIUS' EYES)
When his love he doth espy,
Let her shine as gloriously
As the Venus of the sky.
When thou wak'st, if she be by,
Beg of her for remedy.

(ENTER PUCK)

PUCK
Captain of our fairy band,
Helena is here at hand
And the youth, mistook by me,
Pleading for a lover's fee.
Shall we their fond pageant see?
Lord, what fools this mortals be!

OBERON
Stand aside. The noise they make
Will cause Demetrius to awake.

PUCK
Then will two at once woo one;
This is *my* idea of fun!

(ENTER LYSANDER AND HELENA)

LYSANDER
Why should you think I woo in scorn?
When I vow, I weep, and vows so born
Must bear the badge of faith, and so prove true.
How can this then seem scorn to you?

HELENA
You do advance your cunning more and more.

These vows are *Hermia's*: will you give her o'er?

LYSANDER
I had no judgment when I swore her love.

HELENA
Nor none, I think, now you ignore her love.

LYSANDER
Demetrius loves her, he loves not you.

HELENA
At least Demetrius' love is true.

DEMETRIUS
(WAKING) O Helen, goddess, nymph divine!
To what shall I compare thine eyne?
Crystal is muddy. O how ripe in show,
Thy lips, like cherries, tempting grow!

HELENA
O spite! O hell! I see you all are bent
To set against me for your merriment.
If you were men, as men you are in show,
You would not use a gentle lady so;
To vow, and swear, and superpraise my parts,
When I am sure you hate me with your hearts.
You both are rivals, and love Hermia,
And now both rivals, to *mock* Helena.
A trim exploit, a manly enterprise,
To conjure up tears in a poor maid's eyes.

LYSANDER
You are unkind, Demetrius. Be not so;
For you love Hermia—this you know I know.
And here, with all good will, with all my heart,
In Hermia's love I yield you up my part;
And yours of Helena, to me bequeath,
Whom I do love, and will till death.

DEMETRIUS
Lysander, keep thy Hermia; I will none:
If e're I loved her, all that love is gone.
My heart to her, but as a guest, sojourned,
And now to Helen is it home returned.

LYSANDER
Helen, it is not so.

DEMETRIUS
It is: my love is here.
Look where *thy* love comes: *yonder* is *thy* dear.

(ENTER HERMIA)

HERMIA
Dark night, that doth impair the seeing sense,
It pays the hearing double recompense.
Thou art not by mine eye, Lysander found;
Mine ear, I thank it, brought me to thy sound.
But why unkindly didst thou leave me so?

LYSANDER
Why should he stay whom love doth press to go?

HERMIA
What love could press Lysander from my side?

LYSANDER
Lysander's love, that would have Helena as bride.

HERMIA
You speak not as you think: it cannot be.

HELENA
Lo, she is one of this confederacy!
Now I perceive they have conjoined all three
To fashion this false sport in spite of me.
Injurious Hermia, most ungrateful maid!
Do you conspire freely, or are you *paid*
To bait me with this foul derision;

After all we've shared, is this your decision?
To join with men in scorning your poor friend?
'Tis not maidenly; our sisters vows you rend.
Our sex, as well as I, may chide you for it,
Though I alone feel injury, whilst you adore it.

HERMIA

I am amazed at your passionate plea!
I scorn you not: it seems *you* scorn *me*!

HELENA

Have you not set Lysander, in scorn, apace
To follow me and praise my eyes, my face?
And made Demetrius, your other love there,
Call me goddess, nymph, divine and rare?
Wherefore speaks he thus to her he doth hate?
And wherefore Lysander puts me on his plate,
But by *your* setting on, by *your* consent!

HERMIA

I don't understand what you mean by this rant.

HELENA

Aye, do, persever, counterfeit sad looks,
Hold the sweet jest up, now you've got your hooks
In me. Wink at each other when my back is turned;
This sport, well carried, shows how you have spurned
Me. If you had any pity, manners or grace,
You would not mock me straight to my face.
But fare ye well: 'tis mine own fault, I guess;
By absence or death I shall remedy this mess.

LYSANDER

Stay, gentle Helena! Hear my reply,
My love, my soul: I don't want you to die!

HELENA

O excellent!

HERMIA

Sweet, do not scorn her so.

LYSANDER
Helen, I love thee, by my life, you must know.

DEMETRIUS
I say *I* love thee more than *he* can do.

LYSANDER
If thou say so, withdraw, and prove it too.

DEMETRIUS
Come, let us fight for her, mano à mano.

HERMIA
Lysander, what means this?

LYSANDER
Away, thou bat guano!
Thou cat, thou burr! Vile thing, let loose.

HERMIA
Why are you grown so rude?

LYSANDER
Because you honk like a goose.

HERMIA
Sweet love, do you not jest?

HELENA
Yes, sooth; and so do you.

LYSANDER
'Tis no jest: I love Helena! Be certain that's true.

HERMIA
(TO HELENA)
Why, you canker-blossom! You love thief! Have you come by night
And stolen my love? Get out of my sight!

HELENA
Have you no modesty, no maiden shame?
You counterfeit puppet! I've had enough of this game.

HERMIA
Puppet! Now I see: she hath urged her height,
Made compare of our statures, am I not right?
Are you so high in his esteem because I am low?
Thou painted maypole! Speak, I must know!
Not so low that my nails cannot reach thine eyes!

HELENA
I pray you, gentlemen, don't be deceived by her size,
Let her not hurt me, for though she's but small …

HERMIA
Oh!

HELENA
I have no gift for shrewishness at all.
You may think because she's lower than myself,
That I can match her.

HERMIA
Lower!

LYSANDER
Be not afraid of this elf.

HELENA
Good Hermia, be not so bitter with me.
I ever did love you, never wronged you, you'll see:
I followed Demetrius, though he spurned me the while.
Now I'll bear my folly back to Athens over many a mile,

HERMIA
Why, get you gone. Who hinders you here?

HELENA
A foolish heart, which holds Demetrius dear.

LYSANDER
(TO HELENA) Be not afraid, she shall do you no harm.

DEMETRIUS
No, sir, she shall not, by this strong arm.

HELENA
Though she's but little, she's known to be fierce.

HERMIA
Ha! "Little" again! Thou beanstalk! I'll pierce
That smug armor you wear. Why let her flout me thus?
Nothing but "low" and "little!" Let me at the hussy!

LYSANDER
Get you gone, you dwarf, you acorn, you bead!

DEMETRIUS
Lysander, take not her part. With me here, there's no need.

LYSANDER
Demetrius, if thou dar'st, we will try whose right,
Thine or mine, is most in Helena's sight.
Come, follow!

DEMETRIUS
Follow? Nay, We'll go cheek by jowl.

(EXEUNT LYSANDER AND DEMETRIUS)

HERMIA
This is all your fault, you great hornèd owl.

HELENA
I will not trust you, nor no longer stay;
Your hands are quicker than mine for a fray,
But my legs are longer, to run away.

(EXIT HELENA)

HERMIA
I am amazed, and know not what to say.

(EXIT HERMIA)

OBERON
(TO PUCK) This is *thy* negligence: still thou mistak'st,
Or else wilfully this mess thou mak'st.

PUCK
Believe me, king of shadows, I mistook.
Did you not say I should know the man by his look?
By his Athenian garments? Blameless is my enterprise:
I have anointed an Athenian's eyes;
And so far am I glad it so did sort,
As this their jangling I esteem a sport.

OBERON
Thou see'st these lovers seek a place to fight.
Hie therefore, Robin, overcast the night,
And lead these testy rivals so astray,
As one come not within another's way,
Till o'er their brows, death-counterfeiting sleep
With leaden legs and batty wings doth creep.
Then crush this herb into *Lysander's* eye—
Whose liquor hath this virtuous property:
To take from thence all error with his might,
And make his eyeballs roll with true sight.
When next they wake, all this derision
Shall seem a dream and fruitless vision.
Whiles I in this affair do thee employ,
I'll to my queen and beg her Indian boy;
And then I will her charmèd eye release
From monster's view, and all things shall be peace.

PUCK
My fairy lord, this must be done with haste,
For night's swift dragons cut the clouds full fast.

OBERON
But, not withstanding, make no delay:
We may effect this business yet ere day.

(EXIT OBERON)

PUCK
Up and down, up and down,
I will lead them up and down.
I am feared in field and town;
Goblin, lead them up and down.
Here comes one.

(ENTER LYSANDER)

LYSANDER
Where art thou, proud Demetrius? Speak thou now.

PUCK
(AS DEMETRIUS) Here, villain, drawn and ready. Where art *thou*?

LYSANDER
I will be with thee straight, I follow thy sound.

PUCK
Follow me, then, to plainer ground.

(EXIT LYSANDER. ENTER DEMETRIUS)

DEMETRIUS
Lysander, thou runaway. Speak! Art thou fled?
Or in some bush? Where dost thou hide thy head?

PUCK
(AS LYSANDER) Thou coward, art thou bragging to the stars,
Telling the bushes that thou look'st for wars?
Come, recreant.

DEMETRIUS
Yea, art thou there?

PUCK
Follow my voice: we'll try no manhood here.

(EXEUNT DEMETRIUS AND PUCK. ENTER LYSANDER)

LYSANDER
He goes before me and still dares me on:
When I come where he calls, then he is gone.
The villain is much lighter-heeled than I:
I followed fast, but faster he did fly,
That fallen am I in dark uneven way,
And here will rest me. Come thou gentle day.

(LYSANDER LIES DOWN AND SLEEPS. ENTER PUCK AND DEMETRIUS)

DEMETRIUS
Thou runn'st before me, shifting every place,
And dar'st not stand, nor look me in the face.
Where art thou now?

PUCK
(AS LYSANDER) Come hither, I am here.

DEMETRIUS
Nay then, thou mock'st me. Thou shalt buy this dear
If ever I thy face by daylight see.
Now, go thy way. Faintness constraineth me
To measure out my length on this cold bed:
By day's approach, look to be visited.

(DEMETRIUS LIES DOWN AND SLEEPS. ENTER HELENA)

HELENA
O weary night! O long and tedious night,
Pray, lead me back to Athens; grant some light.
Till then, sleep, that shuts up sorrow's eye,
Steal me awhile from mine own poor company.
(LIES DOWN, SLEEPS)

PUCK
Yet but three? Come one more;
Two of both kinds makes up four.

(ENTER HERMIA)

HERMIA

Never so weary, never so in woe,
I can no further crawl, no further go;
Here will I rest me till the break of day.
Heavens shield Lysander if they mean a fray.
(LIES DOWN, SLEEPS)

PUCK

On the ground,
Sleep sound:
I'll apply
To your eye,
Gentle lover, remedy.
(HE SQUEEZES THE JUICE ON LYSANDER'S EYES)
When thou wak'st,
Thou tak'st
True delight
In the sight
Of thy *former* lady's eye.
Jack shall have Jill;
Naught shall go ill;
And all shall be well.

(EXIT)

ACT IV, scene 1

(THE WOOD; LYSANDER, DEMETRIUS, HERMIA AND HELENA ARE SLEEPING. ENTER TITANIA AND BOTTOM, WITH FAIRIES IN ATTENDANCE; OBERON FOLLOWS)

TITANIA
Come, sit thee down upon this flowery bed,
While I thy amiable cheeks do coy,
And stick musk-roses in thy sleek, smooth head,
And kiss thy fair large ears, my gentle joy.

BOTTOM
Where's Peaseblossom?

PEASEBLOSSOM
Ready.

BOTTOM
Peaseblossom, scratch my head.
Where's Cobweb?

COBWEB
Ready.

BOTTOM
Cobweb, go and kill me a red-
Hipped humble-bee on the top of a thistle,
And bring me the honey-bag; when you've got it, just whistle.
Where's Mustardseed?

MUSTARDSEED
Ready.

MOTH
So is Moth.

MOTH AND MUSTARDSEED
What's your will.

BOTTOM
That you help Peaseblossom to scratch harder still.
I must to the barber, for methinks that my face
Is grown marvelous hairy. Can you get that place?
Ah! That's much better. Pray, don't think it crass;
If a hair tickles, I must scratch, for I'm a tender ass.

TITANIA
Say, sweet love, what thou desir'st to eat.

BOTTOM
Truly, a peck of provender sounds sweet:
To munch some dry oats would make me feel mellow,
And a bundle of hay: sweet hay hath no fellow.

TITANIA
We will fetch thee new nuts from the squirrel's hoard.

BOTTOM
I had rather have dried peas. (YAWNS) Pray, don't think me bored:
A sudden yearning hath come on me to sleep,
Let your people not stir me.

TITANIA
They won't make a peep,
Fairies, away: be gone with your charms.
(EXEUNT FAIRIES)
And I will, like ivy, wind thee in my arms.
Sleep thou. O, how I dote on thee!

BOTTOM
(SNORING) Hee-haw. Hee-haw

TITANIA
O how I love thee!

(THEY SLEEP. ENTER PUCK. OBERON COMES FORWARD)

OBERON
Welcome, Robin. See'st thou this sweet sight?
What think'st thou of thy work.

PUCK
Kinda scary.

OBERON
You're right.
Her dotage now I do begin to pity,
Seeking sweet favors for this fool from the city.
When I did meet her of late in the wood,
She straight gave me the changeling boy.

PUCK
That's good.

OBERON
She sent him to Fairyland, so now I'll undo
This imperfection of her eyes. And *you,*
Gentle Puck, must take the transformèd roof
From off the head of this Athenian goof,
That he may to Athens with this sight unseen.
But first I will release the fairy queen.
(TOUCHES HER EYES WITH AN HERB)
Be as thou wast wont to be;
See as thou wast wont to see:
Dian's bud o'er Cupid's flower
Hath such force and blessed power.
Now, Titania, wake my sweet queen.

TITANIA
My Oberon! What visions I have seen!
Methought I was enamored of an ass.

OBERON
There lies your love.

TITANIA
How came these things to pass?

OBERON
Robin, take off his head; Titania: music call, music

TITANIA
Music, ho! Come one and all!

(ENTER FAIRIES. MUSIC PLAYS. THEY REMOVE THE ASS'S HEAD FROM
BOTTOM)

PUCK
When thou wak'st from this magic sleep,
With thine own fool's eyes wilt thou peep.
(TO OBERON) Fairy king, attend and mark:
I do hear the morning lark.

OBERON
My queen, in silence through this glade,
Trip we together after night's shade.

TITANIA
Come, my lord; and in our flight,
Tell me how it came this night
That I, sleeping, here was found
With this curious mortal on the ground.

(EXEUNT ALL BUT BOTTOM. HUNTING HORNS SOUND OFFSTAGE.
ENTER THESEUS, HIPPOLYTA, EGEUS, PHILOSTRATE)

THESEUS
Go, find out the forester; 'tis the break of day.
My love shall hear the music of my hounds; send them this way.

(EXIT PHILOSTRATE)

HIPPOLYTA
I was once with Hercules in a wood of Crete
Where, with hounds of Sparta, we did meet
Brave Cadmus, and never did I hear
Such baying as when they treed the bear.

THESEUS
My hounds are of the Spartan kind;
But soft, what nymphs are these we find?

EGEUS
My lord, this is my daughter! And this Lysander!
And Demetrius; what make they here, I wonder?
And this is Helena, daughter of old Nedar.
How should we find them here under this cedar?

THESEUS
No doubt they rose up early and came here to mark
The day of our nuptial, then fell asleep in this park.
What think you, Hippolyta?

HIPPOLYTA
My lord, it's as you say.
They faint with excitement for our wedding day.

THESEUS
But speak, good Egeus, let us hear your voice:
Is this not the day Hermia must make her choice?

EGEUS
It is, my lord.

THESEUS
The huntsmen shall them awaken.
(GIVES A SIGNAL: HORNS BLOW OFFSTAGE. THE LOVERS AWAKE)
Good morrow, friends: this is a curious nap you've taken.
I pray you, stand up: your bedclothes are arty.
Now explain how we stumble on this slumber party.

LYSANDER
My lord, I shall reply, though as yet I swear,
I cannot truly say how I came here.
But truly will I speak, and now I do bethink,
I came with Hermia to this wood on the brink
Of Athens; our intent was to flee the gaping maw
Of the most pernicious Athenian law.

EGEUS
Enough, enough! You have enough, my lord,
I beg the law: let him die by the sword!
They would have stolen away, upon my life,

Deprived *me* of a daughter, Demetrius of a wife.

DEMETRIUS
My lord, fair Helen told me of their flight,
And I, in fury, followed them in the night.
But by some power, why I do not know,
My love to Hermia is melted as the snow.
The object and the pleasure of mine eye,
Is only Helena.

HIPPOLYTA
Typical guy.

DEMETRIUS
To her I was betrothed before I changed my mood,
But like a sickness, did I loathe this food.
Now, as in health, come I to my natural taste,
And will evermore be true; I've no more time to waste.

THESEUS
Fair lovers, you are fortunately met,
And of your story we will hear more yet.
Egeus, I overbear you in this fuss,
For in the temple, by and by, along with us
These couples shall eternally be knit.

EGEUS
Knit, great duke?

HIPPOLYTA
Married: Hermia to Lysander, Demetrius to Helena.

EGEUS
Methinks I'm going to puke.

(EXIT EGEUS)

THESEUS
Away with us to Athens. Three and three,
We'll hold a feast in great solemnity.

(EXEUNT THESEUS AND HIPPOLYTA)

DEMETRIUS
Are you sure we are awake? It seems yet to me
That we are asleep, and dream what has come to be.
Was the duke here but now, and bid us to marry?

HELENA
Aye, and Hippolyta.

HERMIA
And my father.

LYSANDER
He looked scary.

DEMETRIUS
Why then, we are awake, or so it seems:
Let us follow, and on the way, recount our dreams.

(EXEUNT DEMETRUIS, HELENA, LYSANDER, HERMIA. BOTTOM AWAKES)

BOTTOM
When my cue comes, call, and I will answer thus:
My next line should be, *"Most fair Pyramus."*
Heigh-ho! Peter Quince! Starveling? Snout!
What? Left me asleep? Stolen hence, you louts.
I have had a rare vision; perhaps it was gas:
Methought I was … methought I had … nay, man is but an ass.
I will get Peter Quince to write a ballad in song:
"Bottom's Dream," he shall call it, and we shall sing along,
Before the duke and company at the end of our play.
But gad, I'm hungry: why am I craving hay?

(EXIT)

ACT IV, scene 2

(ATHENS: A ROOM IN QUINCE'S HOUSE. ENTER QUINCE, FLUTE, SNOUT AND STARVELING)

QUINCE
Have you sent to Bottom's house? Is he come home yet?

STARVELING
He cannot be heard of.

SNOUT
Taken by aliens, I bet.

FLUTE
If he come not home, then the play cannot be,
No man in all Athens can play Pyramus as he.
He hath the best wit of any tradesman in the city.

QUINCE
The best person; and a sweet voice. Ah, it's a pity.

(ENTER SNUG)

SNUG
Masters, the duke is coming from the temple
With lords and ladies: the wedding was ample!
Three couples at least are married this day:
They would have paid good money to see our play.

FLUTE
O sweet bully Bottom! He will rue the cost:
Thus sixpence a day for life he hath lost.

(ENTER BOTTOM)

BOTTOM
Where are these lads? Where are these hearts?

ALL
Bottom!

BOTTOM
My, but I'm glad to see you old farts.

QUINCE
Let us hear, sweet Bottom, what happened to you.

BOTTOM
Not a word; if I say, you'll not believe it's true.
But the duke hath dined, and with his people conferred:
The long and short is, our play is preferred!
Get your things together. Let Thisbe, have long hair,
And the lion long nails: Snug, be sure not to pare
Them. And most, dear actors look to thy breath:
Eat no garlic or onions or we'll breathe them to death.
A comedy is our play:
No more words: away!

(EXEUNT)

ACT V, scene 1

(ATHENS: THE PALACE OF THESEUS. ENTER THESEUS, HIPPOLYTA, PHILOSTRATE, AND ATTENDANTS)

HIPPOLYTA
'Tis strange, my Theseus, what these lovers conceive.

THESEUS
More strange than true. I may never believe
Their curious tale, though it entertains.
Lovers and madmen have such seething brains.

HIPPOLYTA
Yet their story grows to constancy and worth.

(ENTER LYSANDER, HERMIA, DEMETRIUS, HELENA)

THESEUS
Here come the lovers, full of joy and mirth.
Joy, gentle friends, and fresh days of love;
Philostrate: what masques, what dances shall we have,
To wear away the hours before bed?
Come, is there a play, now that we are fed?

PHILOSTRATE
There is, my lord, but hear my voice,
I pray, if you please, make another choice.
(GIVES THESEUS A PAPER TO READ.)

THESEUS
(READS) *A tedious brief scene of Pyramus, and Thisbe, his love.*
Very tragical mirth that, by and by, may move.
Merry and tragical? Tedious and brief?
This is wondrous entertainment. Will it grant some relief?

PHILOSTRATE
It is but ten words, little more than a song,
But truly, though brief, I think it is too long.

THESEUS
Who plays it?

PHILOSTRATE
Hard-handed men of Athens would take their bow;
I swear they've never labored in their minds till now.

THESEUS
We will hear it.

PHILOSTRATE
My lord, it is not for you,
Unless their folly be your sport, and at the end you all boo.

THESEUS
We will hear this play, for nothing can be wrong
When simpleness and duty bring men along.
Go, fetch them in; ladies, sit there beneath.

(EXIT PHILOSTRATE)

HIPPOLYTA
I hope they've bathed.

HERMIA
I hope they've brushed their teeth!

(ENTER PHILOSTRATE)

PHILOSTRATE
So please your grace, the Prologue is ready.

THESEUS
Let him approach.

(FLOURISH OF TRUMPETS. ENTER QUINCE AS THE PROLOGUE)

HELENA
His legs are unsteady.

QUINCE
If we offend, it is with our good will.
We come not to offend, but to show our simple skill.
We do not come as minding to content you;
Our true intent is that you should here repent you.

LYSANDER
He rides his prologue like a colt that's green.

DEMETRIUS
His speech was all tangled. Who's next in this scene?

(EXIT QUINCE. ENTER SNOUT AS THE WALL)

SNOUT
In this same interlude it doth befall
That I, one Snout by name, present a wall;
And such a wall, as I would have you think,
That had in it a crannied hole or chink,
I am that same wall, if you would know,
Through which the lovers whisper, truth is so.

HELENA
Could you desire a wall to give better word?

HERMIA
'Tis the wittiest partition I've ever heard.

(ENTER BOTTOM AS PYRAMUS)

BOTTOM
O grim-looked night! O night with hue so black!
O night! O night! Alack, alack, alack!
And thou, O wall! Sweet wall, show me thy chink
Through which my longing eyes may Thisbe blink.
(SNOUT MAKES A SPACE FOR BOTTOM TO LOOK THROUGH)
Thanks, courteous wall: but O! What do I see?
No Thisbe! Cursed be thy stones for deceiving me.

HIPPOLLYTA
Methinks the wall hath cause to curse right back.

BOTTOM
Madam, he does not, for I am Thisbe-less. Alack!
"Deceiving me" was the cue; Thisbe is to enter now,
And I'm to spy her through the wall, you will see how.

(ENTER FLUTE AS THISBE)

FLUTE

O wall, full often hast thou heard my moans,
My cherry lips have often kissed thy stones,
Thy stones with lime and hair knit up in thee,
That ever part my Pyramus and me.

BOTTOM

I see a voice! Now will I to the crack,
To spy and hear my Thisbe's face cry back.
Thisbe!

FLUTE

My love! Thou art my love, I think.
It's hard to tell what you look like through this chink.

BOTTOM

O, kiss me through the hole of this vile wall!

FLUTE

I kiss the wall's hole … that didn't sound good at all.

BOTTOM

Wilt thou at Ninny's tomb meet me straight away?

FLUTE

Ninus' tomb. I come without delay.

(EXEUNT BOTTOM, FLUTE, SNOUT. ENTER SNUG AND STARVELING)

SNUG

You, ladies, you whose gentle hearts do fear
The smallest monstrous mouse that creeps on floor,
May now perchance both quake and tremble here,
When lion rough in wildest rage doth roar.
Then know that I, one Snug, the joiner am.

THESEUS

A very gentle beast.

HYPPOLYTA

And not a ham.

STARVELING
This lantern doth the crescent moon present,
Myself, the man in the moon, thus heaven-sent.

LYSANDER
Proceed, Moon.

STARVELING
Sir, that's all I have to say.

DEMETRIUS
'Twill serve. Lysander, see: Thisbe comes this way.

(ENTER FLUTE AS THISBE)

FLUTE
This is old Ninny's tomb …

SNUG/STARVELING
Ninus!

FLUTE
Where is my love?

SNUG
Roar!

(FLUTE RUNS OFF, LEAVING THISBE'S MANTLE. THE LION TEARS IT. EXIT SNUG.)

HERMIA
Well roared, Lion!

HELENA
Well run, Thisbe!

HIPPOLYTA
Well shone, Moon! Truly, the moon shines well above.

(ENTER BOTTOM AS PYRAMUS)

BOTTOM
Sweet moon, I thank thee for thy sunny beams,
For by thy gracious, golden, glittering gleams,
I trust to taste of truest Thisbe's sight.
But stay; what's this? O, what a dreadful sight!
How can it be? O dainty duck!
Eyes, do you see? O, what bad luck!
Thy mantle good
Is stained with blood!
A lion vile hath munched my dear!
This mantle shows he lunched right here!
Come sword: with Thisbe I will lie.
Thus, thus, thus I die.

(BOTTOM AS PYRAMUS STABS HIMSELF, DIES. EXIT STARVELING AS MOON.)

HIPPOLYTA
How will Thisbe find him without the moon?

THESEUS
By starlight. She comes: with luck, this play ends soon.

(ENTER FLUTE AS THISBE)

FLUTE
Asleep my love?
What dead, my dove?
O Pyramus, arise!
Speak, speak! Quite dumb?
Dead, dead! A tomb
Must cover thy sweet eyes.
Then farewell, friends,
Thus Thisbe ends,
Come blade, my breast imbrue!
My just desserts …
(STABS HIMSELF)
Ow, that hurts.
Adieu, adieu, adieu.

LYSANDER
Moonshine and Lion must bury the dead.

DEMETRIUS
Aye, and Wall.

BOTTOM
Nay, that cannot be said.
For the wall that parted their fathers is down.
Will you see the epilogue?

THESEUS
Let's leave your epilogue alone.

HERMIA
Thank God.

HELENA
Amen.

HIPPOLYTA
Aye, enough has been said.

THESEUS
Your play needs no excuse now the players are dead.

(EXEUNT BOTTOM AND FLUTE)

LYSANDER
(YAWNS) I fear we shall outsleep the coming day.

DEMETRIUS
I fear we'll have to watch another play.

THESEUS
Lovers, to bed; 'tis almost fairy time
The stroke of midnight hath begun to chime.
A fortnight shall we celebrate our bliss,
In nightly revels.

HIPPOLYTA
Better, we hope, than this.

(EXEUNT. ENTER PUCK, OBERON, TITANIA, WITH FAIRIES)

OBERON
Through the house give glimmering light,
Every elf and every sprite.
By the dead and drowsy fire,
Hop as light as bird from brier.

TITANIA
Now, until the break of day,
Through this house each fairy stray,
And each several chamber bless,
Through this palace, with sweet peace.
Trip away;
Make no stay;
Meet me all by break of day.

(EXEUNT OBERON, TITANIA, AND FAIRIES)

PUCK
If we shadows have offended,
Think but this and all is mended:
That you have but slumbered here
While these visions did appear.
And this weak and idle theme,
No more yielding than a dream,
Gentles, do not reprehend:
If you pardon, we will mend.
And as I am an honest Puck,
If we have unearnèd luck,
Give me your hands, if we be friends,
And Robin shall restore amends.

(LIGHTS OUT)

CURTAIN

ABOUT THE AUTHOR—
RICHARD CARTER

Richard Carter grew up in Portland, Oregon, the son of a doctor and a dancer. Since 1986 he has made his home in the San Juan Islands, between the Olympic Peninsula and the mainland of Washington State.

After graduating from Vassar College and receiving his MFA in playwriting from the University of Washington, Richard's play *Blood and Iron* won the 1993 Jumpstart New Play Competition and was presented by the Seattle Shakespeare Company, and then on the London stage. His musical play, *Winds in the Morning*, received glowing reviews at the 1997 Seattle Fringe Festival, and was selected to inaugurate the Wooden Boat Festival in 2000, at Port Townesend, Washington.

Richard offers his talents in many venues. As Co-founder/Director of the Community Shakespeare Company, he is one of the few playwrights today with the audacity to work *with* Shakespeare. Working in rhyming couplets, updating some of the language, he delivers the best of the Bard for perform-ance by young actors. The adaptations are so authentic that audiences scarcely know they aren't seeing and hearing the original.

Community Shakespeare Company itself breaks new ground. Its mission, "to enrich young lives and cultivate community" uses Shakespeare as the inspira-tion and theatre as the means. Richard's unique adaptations motivate and enchant young actors from 3rd grade up. His leadership skills engage parents, mentors and artists to support and encourage their youth. The result is a dynamic model that can be replicated in schools, organizations, clubs and communities.

Richard and his wife Jeanna live on a small farm where they have been raising their children and practicing sustainable agriculture together since 1988.

NOTES

NOTES

NOTES

NOTES

NOTES

NOTES

978-0-595-48343-3
0-595-48343-7

CPSIA information can be obtained
at www.ICGtesting.com
Printed in the USA
FSOW02n1533260916
25426FS